Stop Identity Theft Today

By John M. Harkins

For the latest information go to:

www.StopIdentityTheftToday.com

ISBN-13:978-1463789220

This book is dedicated to my mom Elaine, who always supported me in every endeavor. She is the reason I'm here at all, and made me who I am today.
My dad John (Chick) who is the kindest and most honest person I have ever met.
I only hope to one day be able to live up to your example.

TABLE OF CONTENTS

CHAPTER 3

CHAPTER 4

CHAPTER 5

INTRODUCTION

The day begins just like any other one normally would. You're on your way to work in the morning and realize you need to make a quick pit stop at the gas station before you run out of fuel completely. You fill up the tank and grab a coffee and newspaper once inside the store. You offer the cashier your credit card and are stunned when she tells you that it has been rejected. As the wave of embarrassment rushes over you, you fumble around in your pockets for enough cash to cover the entire bill. On the way out you stop at the ATM to replace the money you had in your pocket and to your horror the screen tells you that your account has insufficient funds. Panicked now, you arrive at the office and immediately check your online credit card and bank statements.

Your checking account is in overdraft which means there must be some kind of mistake as you know there was enough in there for the next mortgage payment and then some. Your credit card statement shows thousands upon thousands of dollars worth of purchases over the last two weeks that you know you didn't make. When you finally call the bank to find out what's going on they pass you over to a supervisor who tells you that the loan you recently applied for has been denied. Because you've applied for credit at a number of other places within the last month they aren't comfortable in extending a loan to you based on your current debt load.

With your head spinning and thoughts coming at you a million a minute you finally realize…you have just become the latest victim of Identity Theft.

CHAPTER 1

WHAT IS IDENTITY THEFT?

As the quickest growing crime in America, identity theft affects approximately 7 –10 million people every single year.

Simply put, identity theft is the act of using someone else's personal information, or their actual identity for personal gain. Frighteningly it happens without you even knowing it and once you have become aware of it, in most cases the damage has already been done.

Types of Identity Theft

Although there are many different methods that one can utilize to rip someone off in an identity theft type scam, there are really only two basic types of actual identity theft.

The first of these is generally the easiest and most basic way for thieves to achieve their objective. An example of Account takeover is when a thief gets hold of your actual physical credit card, or perhaps just the card number and expiration date, using it to purchase services or products. This works out extremely well for the thief, as the credit card owner doesn't usually notice the additional purchases until they either receive their monthly statement in the mail or have attempted to use the card and found that it has reached the maximum limit allowed.

The second type of identity theft is called, or what is otherwise known as "true name fraud". In order for a thief to be successful at application fraud, they must have access to a good deal of your personal information such as your Social Security Number (SSN), full name, address, place of work, salary, driver's license number, date of birth etc. Of course not all of these pieces of information would be necessary for a thief to get away with application fraud but certainly a combination of some of the above would be required.

It Can Affect Anyone

Like many, you may assume that identity theft only happens to those people who might be a bit more careless when it comes to safeguarding personal information. Or perhaps you are of the mindset that because you don't really have a lot of money in your personal account or don't have credit cards with large spending limits, that identity theft thieves wouldn't necessarily target someone like yourself. Well, make no mistake about it; identity theft can happen to anyone, including you! Basically, if you have an identity (and we hope that you do) then you are susceptible.

The size of your financial worth does not matter, nor whether you rent or own your home, nor whether you have exceptional credit or bad. The fact is still this, if you are reading this right now then you have an identity and because of that you are certain to have one, if not many of the following: a name, a bank account, a credit card, a telephone, a SSN, a job, a birth date, an email and internet account, a mailbox, an address, and the list goes on and on. And I hate to break this to you my friend but here's my point, it only takes one of the above pieces of information to fall into the wrong hands and you too, like millions of others can become a victim of identity theft.

Not As Difficult As You Think

Still think it's not that easy for someone to get your personal information? Well let's not be naïve about this, it's not as difficult as you think it is. Take a moment to think about all of the companies, organizations, businesses and online sites that might have access to ANY of your personal information. Think about all of the people who handle your mail before it reaches its intended destination.

Think about all of that extremely personal information you include on your resume when you're job hunting and that you will send it out to who knows how many companies? Your complete work history, name, contact information and possibly references are all included in your resume! What about where you work now? They have access to more of your personal information than even what your spouse or parents might have! Now think about all of the people who your employer passes that information onto, such as the insurance company, and not only your own bank but their bank as well, and let's not forget the company that processes payroll! The list is endless and in just a little while we will discuss all the ways in which you can protect yourself against identity theft. For now however, let's take a look at all of the methods in which thieves might use to access your personal information.

CHAPTER 2

METHODS OF IDENTITY THEFT

As we start to discuss all of the various ways in which identity theft can occur, you may begin to realize just how vulnerable you might be. Now remember, the intention of this book is certainly not to frighten the living daylights out of you, nor is it to turn you into a paranoid, crazy person who decides that they don't trust anyone anymore and that they now must cancel all of their credit cards, close out their bank account and hide all their cash under the bed mattress in an attempt to leave a paperless trail in everything that they do. The actual intention of this book is quite simple. Let's make you aware of how identity theft does occur so that you can walk away with the knowledge of what precautions to take so that it doesn't ever affect you. And if the worst-case scenario does present itself and you do become a victim, this book will ensure that you are not at a loss as to how to deal with it, what actions you must take to correct the problem, or how stop it before it gets worse.

Dumpster Diving

Imagine for a moment it's that time of month we all detest – time to pay the bills. As you sort through the pile of mail on your desk you first throw out all of that junk mail that you receive from every store you have ever been to who has put you on their mailing list (you know - so that they can make you aware of upcoming sales and promotions etc). Oh yes, and we can't forget about all the credit card and loan companies that want to let you know they have generously pre-approved you for a new credit card or loan. Let's face it; those are probably destined for the garbage or recycling bin as well. Once we have finally gotten to the task of actually paying those nasty bills, many of us discard those statements also. Bills that have account numbers, credit limits, contact information and all other types of personal information, are all very accessible in your garbage can as it sits waiting patiently on the side of the road all ready for the garbage truck to come by in the morning and collect it.

Don't think for a minute that thieves have too much pride to go digging through your trash can to find what they're after, because believe me, they don't! If they happen to grab your entire bag of trash on the same week that you paid your bills then they just hit the personal information lottery! Think of all the damage they could do with everything you threw away by opening up new credit card accounts with those pre-approved notices you received. All they'd have to do is respond to the notices, tell the credit company that you've moved and provide a mailing address that they could access and boom…thousands and thousands of dollars in debt built up in no time at all, debt that you are not likely to become aware of for months.

Mail Stealing

If they're bold enough to steal your garbage from the side of the road then you certainly shouldn't put it past them to steal your mail. Of course it may be a bit easier for them if you have one of those road side mailboxes so that they appear less conspicuous than they would walking up to your door. Remember though, these guys are smart and have probably been doing this for a long time. Printing off some bogus flyers and posing as someone delivering them so that they can more easily approach your front door and open up your mail box isn't exactly rocket science. Your mailbox can provide them with newly issued credit or bank cards, a new batch of checks for your personal or business accounts, investment reports, insurance statements, tax information and bank statements.

Shoulder Surfing

How many times per day or week do you use your ATM card to pay for purchases or use a banking machine to deposit or withdraw funds? Thieves have become very skilled and discreet about watching people key in PIN numbers and even from a distance can determine your personal ID number. You may be thinking right now that a thief really can't do any damage with your PIN if they don't have your actual card so what's the big deal? Well then, you obviously aren't familiar with "skimming" so please, read on...

ATM Skimming

ATM skimming is a very real and very present threat in the world of identity theft scams. Thieves can create very inexpensive, home-made skimming devices that attach to the ATM card reader, thus allowing them to collect hundreds or thousands of card numbers in a very short period of time. There are two different types of devices that are commonly used: one that interferes with the customer's ability to actually use the ATM machine successfully, and one that doesn't. The type of device that interferes with the normal operating ability of the machine is generally a bit easier to recognize.

Thieves will look for an ATM that they can alter the face of and build an attachment for. In some cases, they may use a fabricated metal container of sorts that would fit onto the existing machine and may have a small laptop computer inside that would prompt the customer to use a touch screen instead of the machines actual keypad. It may also offer an alternate card reader next to it. With a small, undetectable camera recording your PIN number as you enter it attached to or near the ATM, the thief would have all the information he needed to access your account once you had finished attempting to process your transaction.

However, because you were actually using a fake card reader and prompting system, the final screen may read something like, "Thank you for using National Bank (or whatever type of banking machine you were using). There has been a malfunction."

The type of skimmer that would not interfere with your transaction process would most commonly be found on banking machines that require you to swipe your card through an external, raised slot. Not on those where you manually slide your card into the actual machine in which the reader head would be buried inside the unit. This is because the external readers are much more accessible to thieves and the skimmer can be placed directly overtop of the actual reader strip. You as a customer can still make your withdrawal and the thief still gets your number. These types of devices are very difficult, if not impossible for the untrained eye to identify. ATM banking machines are not the only devices at risk when it comes to skimming. A skimmer can be attached to any type of system with an external reader, such as the one you use to pay your bill at the grocery store, gas station, department store or restaurant.

Check Fraud

Identity thieves will stop at nothing to take control of your available cash and credit, even if it means setting up a little counterfeit scam from the comforts of their own home by recreating checks in your name on their own computer. Alternately, those industrious types who have been fortunate enough to get their hands on a check that has already been fully written out and signed, may use cleaning solvent to remove the name of whom the check was originally made payable to and will put their own name in it's place. Other thieves who already have access to certain personal information may choose to open up a checking account in your name, using it to write bad checks and accumulating a load of debt that will appear on your credit report.

Telephone Service Fraud

Identity thieves aren't only after just your cold hard cash, they'll scam you in whatever way possible and take you for everything they can. Just as important as safeguarding your ATM or credit cards, remember that your calling card can also be worth a fortune in services. Think of the enormous long distance charges that could accumulate over a month's time and how shocking that bill will be when you finally receive it! With access to a little bit of your personal information, identity thieves can even establish new cellular telephone service in your name.

Telephone Scams

How many times every week do you receive phone calls from a charity of some sort, asking you for your financial support? Or perhaps the call is from a marketing firm requesting your assistance in completing a survey. Now this is not to say that everyone calling you claiming to be with a charitable organization or marketing firm is really a scam artist looking to rip you off, but certainly the possibility exists. Any caller asking you for personal information such as credit cards or Social Security Numbers should raise a red flag for you. And, any charity truly requiring your financial help will be more than happy to send you a package of information that will provide you with many options of how you can make your donation. It is not necessary for you to give out credit card information at that time. Additionally, any marketing firm conducting a survey does not actually require your SSN unless of course their goal is to rip you off!

Credit Card Theft

We did talk earlier a little bit about how identity thieves will use your actual credit card or other information to purchase products or services, but they don't just stop there, let's look at how they take it one step further. Resourceful thieves will take almost extreme measures by visiting the local post office and in your name, request a change of address for your mail so that they can access all of your bills and account numbers. By the time you realize that you haven't received your monthly bills they will have already accumulated a substantial amount of debt and charges to your credit cards.

Thieves can also access your credit card number or other personal information when payments or purchases are made through either unsecured or fraudulent web sites.

Phishing

Before you get too confused let me clarify right now that this is not in any way related to the kind of "fishing" you do out on the lake, in your boat with a pole and bait. However it does use the same theory. This is the kind of phishing where identity thieves plant bait and lure unsuspecting victims into providing confidential and personal information. Phishing scams have been around forever, what has changed about them is simply the route in which the scam is delivered. Before the computer, phishers used the telephone, however in this day and age the vehicle of choice is the internet.

Have you ever received an email with a message similar to any of the following?

- We suspect an unauthorized transaction on your account. To ensure that your account is not compromised, please click the link below and confirm your identity.

- During our regular verification of accounts, we couldn't verify your information. Please click here to update and verify your information.

- eBay requires you to update your account information.

- PayPal account renewal required

- Bank of America security alert

- $20 Reward Survey, Chase Manhattan Bank

- Please update your bank account

- JC Penny gift card offer confirmation

- American Red Cross/Hurricane Katrina Relief

These are all examples of actual phishing scam messages that are either sent via email or by way of pop-up messages. The phisher will often include in the message the name of a well-known, reputable business, organization, government agency or financial institution that you perhaps deal with. The goal is in attempting to give the message an air of legitimacy.

Some of them may even go, as far in threatening you with severe consequences as a result if you do not respond. Messages will ask you to update, validate or confirm particular personal or account information and will direct you to a website in order to complete the process. When you click on the link for the website it may very well look fully legitimate, however it is not.

It may appear to look like the link for eBay, PayPal, The Bank of America, or whatever source the email claims to be coming from.

Remember, these guys are good and this is not just a hobby for them, this is a profession. Their aim is to deceive you and they will do whatever they have to do in order for you to believe the legitimacy of their scheme.

CHAPTER 3

PREVENTING IDENTITY THEFT

Let's check in to see how you're doing before we go any further. That was a lot of information to absorb and for someone who's new to the whole world of Identity Theft it was likely very overwhelming.

You're doing really well though and I'm proud of you! You made it through the most difficult part of this book. You learned all about the scariness of ID theft and the many forms it can take and look, you're still here. Now it's time for your reward. The first portion of this book may have caused you to feel helpless, frightened or without power against the enormity of the problem. Now however it's time for you to learn that there is something you can do about it. Knowledge is power and here is where you become EMPOWERED!

Protecting Your Mail

Remember how we talked about thieves that would steal your mail from the garbage and even from your own mailbox? Well don't let them! Make sure that every single piece of mail with any kind of identifying information on it is shredded before you throw it away. Simply tearing it into a few pieces is not adequate protection. This only provides the thief with a fairly basic jigsaw puzzle to your most valued information. Invest in a small shredder for your home. These are very inexpensive especially when you consider that the minimal cost of the item could save you hundreds or thousands of dollars in the long run, not to mention a huge headache. If you can't purchase one yourself then take your mail to work with you and use the shredder in your office.

A locked mailbox will not completely guarantee your protection from identity thieves but it certainly may help in dissuading their attempts to steal your mail. Look into purchasing a mailbox that has a slot in the top for the mail to be slid into but where you need a key to actually remove it. This way, if your mailbox is broken into you will at least know it right away and will perhaps be able to notify creditors, banks and other companies before any real damage is done.

Bills always tend to arrive on a monthly basis like clockwork so pay attention to billing cycles. If a credit card or utility bill does not arrive on time, contact the company to make sure it has not been redirected.

Safeguard Your PIN and ATM/Credit Card

You know that moment in the store when you're just about to pay for your purchases using your ATM card and the thought crosses your mind that you should probably use your free hand to cover the keypad so that no one can see the number you're punching in? But then you don't do it because you think that the cashier or person behind you in line will just think that you're being silly and over reacting – I mean, it's not like you have the code to the universe right? Wrong! It may not be the code to THE universe but it is the code to YOUR universe. Who cares what other people think or how you may look to them – you need to protect that code because it is the key to your mortgage and bill payments, to your children's education fund, to your next family vacation and to the food, clothing and supplies that sustain your family!

Make sure you are aware of where your ATM or credit card is at all times. When you hand your card to the cashier or to the waiter at the restaurant, is that card ever out of your sight? Does it disappear for a moment underneath the counter while it's in their hand or is it left to sit on the far side of the counter until the transaction is approved? You may not be able to prevent the fact that the waiter needs to take your card with him to process it, but you can certainly be more aware of situations like this when they do occur.

Now that you know what ATM skimming is you can be more aware of machines that don't seem quite right. If a machine looks as though it has been altered or tampered with in any way simply do not use it. If a machine has a sign posted on it telling you that the ATM instructions have changed or that you should swipe your card "here" first before inserting it into the reader, or something to that effect then it's not a machine you should be using.

No bank is ever going to post instructions such as these:

- Don't give your PIN to anyone

- Beware of people who try to "help" you at bank machines

- If your card is not returned to you once you have completed the transaction or pressed the cancel button, contact your financial institution immediately

- Check your bank and credit card statements regularly and carefully to make sure that there are no unauthorized transactions

Protect Your Personal Information

It's great to have a trusting nature and all but it is possible to sometimes be too trusting. Don't provide anyone with information that they have no need for regardless of what they claim their reason is for requiring it. Always keep in mind what one can do with a few key pieces of information such as your SSN or driver license number.

- Be careful of who around you might be listening to your conversation when you are speaking either on the telephone or to someone in person and are providing them with personal information.

- Refrain from including your date of birth, SSN or drivers license number on job applications or resumes

- Question any business or company who asks for your SSN

Avoiding a Phishing Scam

A very large portion of the population today has access to the internet and email within their own homes. Any of us who aren't so technologically advanced at home, yet who work in an office type environment are likely to be pretty internet savvy at work. This means that an awful lot of us are susceptible to being sucked into those phishing scams. However you can avoid falling into this trap by playing it smart.

- Use anti-virus software and a firewall to prevent phishing emails from tracking your internet activities

- Never email personal or financial information – email is not a secure method of transmission

- Immediately delete any emails that appear to be fraudulent

- Be cautious about opening any attachments or downloading files from email regardless of who is sending them

- Do not reply to or open any links that are provided in phishing emails

- If you are concerned about an account that is referred to in an email, you are best to physically telephone the company whom the email is claiming to be from and ask them personally if there is a problem

- Look for poor grammar and misspelled words in phishing emails

- Legitimate businesses and financial institutions are not likely to ask for personal information via email

- Emails that do not address you by your full name but instead sometimes just by your email address are a tip off

- When you must provide financial or other sensitive information online be sure that the site you are using is secure. Look for a lock icon on the status bar or a website that begins with https: (the "s" stands for secure).

Additional Preventative Measures

I think you're probably getting the point now. There are many things that you can do when it comes to protecting yourself from becoming a victim of identity theft. It may not be possible to follow every single piece of advice that this book provides and that's okay. The key here is awareness.

Here is why awareness is so critically important. Have you ever been really afraid to do something completely new, or been extremely intimidated by something that you knew very little about? Well I certainly have and I'm sure that quite literally everyone else in this world has been as well at one point or another. In fact, it's simply human nature to fear the unknown and I believe that the same can be said for something like identity theft. Before you knew what it was all about the entire idea of it was scary, but now you're becoming more familiar with it and you are gaining the tools and knowledge that will allow you to effectively deal with it.

Let's provide you with even more knowledge now and suggest a few more ways to prevent identity theft from occurring.

- Contact the Better Business Bureau in your area if you receive suspicious phone calls or emails in regards to a particular organization or business

- Ensure that all of your accounts require passwords in order for changes or inquiries to be made to them

- When choosing, make sure you pick difficult passwords (do not use family or pet names etc), do not use the same passwords for each account and memorize them rather than writing them down

- Carry only the cards that you actually need, this includes your Social Security card

- When you are asked for personal information ask why it is needed, who will have access to it, how it is to be used and how they will protect that information from others

- Access your credit report on an annual basis to make sure that it is accurate and that there has not been an accumulation of unauthorized debt
- Inquire as to the policy of those businesses that you do business with when it comes to the discarding of personal/financial information

- Contact the three major credit reporting agencies to place a security alert on your file – this will ensure that you are contacted prior to the opening of any new credit cards under your name

CHAPTER 4

WHAT TO DO WHEN ID THEFT OCCURS

Even with all of the precautions and care you've taken to protect yourself from those spineless and despicable thieves, somehow and someway they found a way to the inside…to the inside your personal and financial life that is. Now don't be too hard on yourself.

I know that you're saying to yourself right now, "I did everything I could possibly do. I took the time to make myself aware and educate myself on the facts and this still happened…why?" Well, unfortunately sometimes there is no real answer to the question why, it just is what it is. You have to keep in mind that these perpetrators are professionals and they will stop at nothing to achieve their goal.

Just like you go to work everyday and perform your job with the proficiency and skills that you have acquired, so do they. Their job everyday is to rip off honest, hardworking and innocent people such as you and I. It's not fair and it never will be. They have made a huge mess of your life and you are the one who is stuck with the task of picking up the pieces and turning things right again. Sometimes you can build that fence higher, make the bridge more difficult to cross and even fill the moat with alligators, but inevitably there will always remain a weak and penetrable spot. Identity thieves are adept at looking for and seeking out those particular spots.

The most important thing for you to keep in mind right now is that regardless of how much damage was done and how bad the situation looks at present, it could always be worse. Think about what would have happened had you not already been so familiar with how identity theft works. You may not have been able to prevent it but you certainly knew how to recognize the fact that it was happening to you.

The signs were there and you didn't just dismiss them, as many others would have this early in the process. Maybe you noticed that your credit card statements had not arrived at the time of month that they generally should have. Perhaps during regular review of your bank statements you noticed some unusual transactions that you had not made.

Maybe in looking more closely at the checks that had been returned to you from the bank you realized that one or several of them were made payable to an unknown individual, tipping you off to the fact that some of your checks had been stolen. Whatever the situation, you are to be congratulated for catching on so quickly.

You now have the ability to stop this thief cold in his tracks and prevent him/her from violating your privacy any further. This could have gone on for months and months or perhaps even years and in the process could have resulted in hundreds or thousands of dollars worth of built up debt and a lifetime of rebuilding the reputable line of credit you once had.

The task at hand now is to deal with the damage that has been done and prevent any additional from occurring. You may be feeling a little bit overwhelmed right now at the many thoughts that are swirling around in your head of all the things that need to be done immediately. However, just try to be calm, breathe deeply and you will get through this.

Let's take some time right now to go through a complete and thorough task list. Keep in mind, that depending on the type of identity theft you have been the victim of, not all of these actions may be necessary. Yet it is important to cover as many bases as possible. Although your thief for instance may have only accessed one of your credit cards, the possibility exists for them to have gained a lot more of your personal information with that one card.

Steps to Take in Recovering Your Identity and Line of Credit

- Ensure that you report the crime to the police right away and request a copy of the police report as you may be required to provide it as proof of the crime when you are later contacting the businesses and organizations you need to deal with

- Document all of the steps that you take, names of all the people whom you deal with and any expenses you incur in re-establishing your credit and clearing your name

- Cancel all of your credit cards and have new ones issued

- Close all of your bank accounts and open new ones

- Order new bank machine and telephone calling cards and change all of your passwords

- If your passport has been stolen contact the passport office

- If your mail has been diverted, contact the post office

- Apply for a new driver's license

- Advise all of your utility companies (including home telephone and cellular service providers) that someone using your name may attempt to open unauthorized new accounts

- Contact the fraud departments for each of the three major credit bureaus to ensure that your credit reports reflects the case of identity theft and follow up with them after a 3 month period to ensure that someone has not tried again to use your identity. This will also ensure that your permission is received prior to opening any new types of credit accounts

- Ask the credit bureaus for copies of your credit report so that you may carefully review them and ensure that no fraudulent loans or accounts exist

- Notify your bank of stolen or misplaced checks, ensure a stop payment order is placed on them and contact the major check verification companies requesting that they notify retailers using their databases not to accept the lost or stolen checks

- Contact the Federal Trade Commission who will assist you as a victim by providing information that will help you to resolve any financial issues or other problems as a result of your identity theft

CHAPTER 5

YOUR LIABILITY AS THE VICTIM OF ID THEFT

The question you have probably been asking yourself throughout this entire book is…"What is my liability in this situation"? Well unfortunately that answer is fairly complex and is dependant on the type of identity theft that has occurred, as well as the timeliness in which you have responded and taken action to correct the problem. In some cases, victims are able to identify and act on the problem quickly resulting in very minimal financial loss. Other particular situations have not worked out quite so well and have resulted in substantial financial debt and a very poor credit rating, which can take years and years to repair.

Let me tell you about a few specific cases of identity theft in where the victim truly ended up as the injured party in more ways than one.

Actual Identity Theft Victim Cases

A gentleman in San Diego, California (we'll call him John Jones), encountered an identity thief who opened a PayPal account under John's name and filtered $7,600 from John's Bank of America account into the forged PayPal account. The incident occurred during July and August of 2002 but because John had been traveling he did not notice the money was actually missing until January of 2003. He contacted his bank and was informed that because he had failed to notify the bank within 60 days of the occurrence there was nothing they could do for him. By that time all of the money, with the exception of $2,100 still remaining in the PayPal account had been spent. PayPal returned the remaining sum to John but he was still out $5,000. John sued both PayPal and Bank of America in small claims court, pleading that PayPal should have notified him immediately upon discovering the fraud. Bank of America counter argued that it is the customer's responsibility to regularly check bank statements and ensure their accuracy. In the end John walked away with a settlement from each of the firms, however was still out approximately $500 as a result. His yearlong battle to turn things right was extensive, time consuming and frustrating.

An elderly woman in Seattle, Washington (we'll call her Jane Doe), was the victim of a telemarketing scam in December of last year. Jane provided her checking account information to the caller and later found that her account had been cleaned of $800, leaving her overdrawn by $300. When her December Social Security check was deposited the Bank of America withdrew $300 of it to cover the overdraft. Jane was left with barely enough money for food and rent and was forced to "skip" Christmas that year. By February the Bank of America had returned some of the money to her and was continuing to work with her to repair the situation.

A retired California couple (let's call them the Smiths), were also the victims of identity theft in April of 2001. The Smiths, when attempting to refinance their home mortgage discovered that there was $75,000 in unsettled debts on an account that they had held with this particular mortgage company over a year ago. This was very strange, as they knew they had settled their debt and closed that account a year earlier. It seems that an identity thief had re-opened the account and switched the original mailing address to one in Houston Texas, which is why the Smiths had never received any bills or statements for that account. After three months of phone calls and paperwork, the Smiths had finally received confirmation from the mortgage company that they were not being held responsible for the debt. However, in December of 2003 the Smiths received a notice from the mortgage company's Financial Services Network that they were being sued for $75,000 plus attorney's fees for their negligence in not discovering and reporting the identity theft in a timely manner, and thus causing injury to the mortgage company. The Smiths hired a lawyer who specialized in identity theft cases and who was eventually successful in convincing the company to drop the lawsuit. The remaining bad news in this case is that the lawsuit was dropped "without prejudice", meaning that the firm could resurrect the case in the future should they choose to do so. The Smiths endured this nightmare for almost a three-year period and still the possibility of future incidents hang over their head.

This last case that I want to share with you is more than horrific but thankfully took place prior to the United States Congress making the act of Identity Theft a federal crime. Although this is certainly not something that this victim is thankful for in anyway, but we can take comfort in knowing that an incident like this would result in a very different ending in today's times. In this particular situation the criminal who was already a convicted felon accumulated more than $100,000 in credit card debt, applied for and obtained a federal home loan, bought homes, motorcycles and handguns in the victims name. The criminal went so far as to even call the victim and taunt him with the fact that because identity theft was not a federal crime he could continue his charade for as long as he wanted to and nothing would happen. The criminal eventually filed for bankruptcy in the victim's name while in the meantime the victim spent over $15,000 and four years in efforts to clear his name and re-establish his credit. In the end the criminal was not reprimanded in any way and never paid back one cent to the victim. His only punishment was serving a brief sentence due to the fact that he made a false statement when he purchased his firearm.

How Will You be Affected?

By now you are likely beginning to see very clearly why it is that I keep preaching to you over and over how critically important the issue of awareness and knowledge is when it comes to identity theft. And, after looking at the three case studies I just shared, you can see now more than ever the enormity of the consequences when you do not monitor your credit and financial statements. If you have been paying close attention throughout this book then hopefully many thoughts have been running through your mind of how the situations could have been prevented when we discussed the stories of the individuals who were victims of identity theft. You may have been thinking back to all of the prevention tips that you have been provided with, and which of those would have been helpful in each of these cases had those victims had the knowledge that you now have.

Let's now spend some time looking at what your liability is as the victim of identity theft depending on the specific situation.

Credit Card Liability

If you have been the victim of credit card identity theft you may take some comfort in the fact that credit card liability is limited to $50. If you actually report the credit card lost prior to it being used then you cannot be held accountable for any unauthorized charges that occur after that time. However, if the identity thief uses your card before you have reported it missing or stolen then the maximum amount you will be charged is $50. The same rule applies even if the credit card is used at an ATM to withdraw cash.

Beware of telemarketers who call to sell you "loss protection" insurance for your credit cards. These callers may trick you into believing that should your card be lost or stolen that you will be solely responsible for any charges made to it if you do not have the "loss protection".

ATM and Debit Card Liability

Unfortunately ATM and debit cards do not offer nearly the amount of protection that credit cards do in cases of loss or theft. It is in cases like these where time is truly of the essence and in the end it is very beneficial for you to keep proper track of your statements and card usage. When and if you do notice a discrepancy it is in your best interest to report it immediately to the issuing office. If you are fortunate in that you report the missing card prior to it being used then your financial institution cannot hold you liable for any unauthorized use. If you report the incident within two business days of the loss your liability is capped at $50. In cases where the report is made anywhere after two business days and before sixty days you will be held liable for up to $500 of what the identity thief stole from you. If a victim were to wait more than sixty days, they could potentially lose every single cent that was stolen prior to reporting the card missing. However, we know for a fact that this last scenario couldn't possibly happen to you. You're much too smart and well informed to let this happen especially knowing everything that you know now…right?

Check Liability

In most cases you would not be held liable in the situation of forged checks as the majority of States hold the bank liable. However, this doesn't mean that you have no responsibility in the situation. If you are negligent in notifying the bank within a reasonable amount of time that a check had been lost or stolen, or if you fail to monitor your account for unauthorized transactions then the liability may well rest with you.

It's Your Responsibility

Don't fool yourself into believing that when or if identity theft hits you that the responsibility lies with someone else. It certainly may not be your fault when it happens but you will be held accountable if you allow it to continue and just assume that someone else will look after the mess. It's your responsibility to protect your financial fate, security and credit rating. If you don't do it, no one else will and you will surely be taken advantage of. Take precautions, monitor your accounts and act quickly if identity theft does occur. A prompt and efficient response to the matter is the best way for you to minimize your loss.

Liability Agreements

How often do you sign up for new services, credit cards, loans or accounts? Now tell me how many times you actually read through the entire liability agreement that accompanies that card or service. That's what I thought, like most of us you may not take the time to read through those seemingly endless agreements that are filled with so much technical and legal mumbo jumbo that it just makes your head hurt.

And what about those online agreements? Do you generally scroll down to the bottom of them without reading a word, click the "I agree" button and then hit "continue"? Many of us do and unfortunately this is where we run into trouble later on once we have become an identity thief victim. I understand that at the time it may seem tedious and unnecessary to read through those agreements but perhaps in the future you might give it a second thought. Additionally, how familiar are you with your liability responsibilities in regards to your current bank accounts, credit cards, debit cards, telephone and cellular service providers, utility providers and online PayPal, eBay and other similar accounts? Not too sure, are you? This might be the perfect opportunity to go back and look at those agreements once again. You may decide that having some of those particular accounts are not worth the price you may have to pay should you one day find yourself in unfortunate circumstances such as those that our three case studies did. Hopefully though as a result of your research you are able to determine that the financial institutions and various companies that you deal with place you as their customer, on the top of their priority list ensuring that you are well protected against identity theft incidences.

CONCLUSION

Much has been covered on the topic of identity theft throughout this book and hopefully it has been successful in answering all of your questions, clarifying any misconceptions or myths and in providing you with an enlightened understanding of the issues involved in identity theft.

We have conquered not only what identity theft is and how it occurs but also, how you can have a hand in preventing it and knowing what to do when or if it does affect you. The sad reality remains however that no matter how many precautions you take it is never possible to be fully immune to identity thieves.

Even when you've done everything possible the threat still exists and always will. The best that you can do for yourself and your family is to protect what you are capable of protecting and arm yourself with the knowledge that will help you deal with whatever else it happens to be that may come along at some later point in life. Often you are not only relying on just your own actions and methods of protection but also those of the companies whom you have entrusted with your personal information.

It's very similar to when a parent tells their son or daughter who has just received their driver's license that they need to be careful on the road. The child generally responds with, "Mom, dad, I am a safe driver, don't worry about me". The parent then tells the child, "It's not your driving that I'm worried about, it's the other people on the road that concern me." The fact is, you just can't control the actions, mistakes or oversights of others. You are forced to put your faith into them and into their capabilities. You must trust that they are as concerned about your privacy and in protecting it as you are. You must believe that they will act with due diligence in taking every step possible on your behalf to prevent an act of identity theft against you.

However, sometimes those people fail, they let us down and they put us at great risk.

Here are some actual headlines from major news sources of cases where very well known and very large institutions have compromised the privacy of their customers.

- ChoicePoint: More ID theft warnings…company says criminals able to obtain almost 140,000 names, addresses and other information.

- American Online has confirmed that hackers have illegally compromised an undisclosed number of its member accounts

- LexisNexis, a worldwide provider of legal and business data, announced yesterday that information about 32,000 consumers was fraudulently gathered in a series of incidents.

- For the second time in about a year, the credit reporting company Equifax Canada Inc. has suffered a security breach that has given criminals access to personal financial information.

- AOL breach gives spam fight a twist…The security breach, believed to be one of the worst of its kind, is the latest twist in the proliferation of spam: a rogue employee supplying a subscriber list for profit.

- Bank of America says at least 1.2 million federal employee credit card accounts may be exposed to theft or hacking

Make an effort to be familiar with those businesses that you deal with and ask them what steps and measures they take in protecting you? You have entrusted them with your personal information and financial matters, which means you have every right to expect nothing less than all of their efforts in protecting your privacy.

You also have every right to hold them accountable for any breach of privacy that does occur. Remember, these are the same companies that are telling you to protect yourself from identity theft. But are they taking the same care when it comes to your protection? You deserve to know, so ask them. There are many competing companies out there that would love your business, and if the ones that you are working with currently can't satisfy you with the kinds of answers that these important questions deserve, be confident and know that someone in some other place certainly can.

RESOURCES

Use the following list of resources to help you in taking action if you have become an identity theft victim.

Credit Card Contact Information

Visa – (800) 847-2911

Mastercard – (800) 622-7747

American Express – (800) 554-2639

Credit Bureau Fraud Departments

TransUnion

Fraud Victim Assistance Department

Phone: (800) 680-7289

Fax: (714) 447-6034

P.O. Box 6790

Fullerton, CA 92634-6790

Equifax

Consumer Fraud Division

Phone: (800) 525-6285 or (404) 885-8000

Fax: (770) 375-2821

P.O. Box 740241

Atlanta, GA 30374-0241

Experian

Experian's National Consumer Assistance

Phone: (888) 397-3742

P.O. Box 2104

Allen, TX 75013

Check Verification Companies

Check Rite – (800) 766-2748

Chex Systems – (800) 328-5121

CrossCheck – (800) 552-1900

Equifax-Telecredit – (800) 437-5120

NPC – (800) 526-5380

SCAN – (800) 262-7771

Tele-Check – (800) 366-2425

REFERENCES

Identity Theft Resource Center

www.idtheftcenter.org

Federal Trade Commission

http://www.ftc.gov/index.html

Bankrate

www.bankrate.com

Office of the Privacy Commissioner of Canada

http://www.privcom.gc.ca/index_e.asp

MSNBC

http://msnbc.msn.com/id/4264051

Privacy Rights Clearing House

http://www.privacyrights.org/index.htm

Fight Identity Theft

www.fightidentitytheft.com

Protect My Info

http://what-is-identity-theft.com

Computer World

http://www.computerworld.com

All Free Info.com

http://all-free-info.com/phishing

United States Department of Justice

http://www.usdoj.gov/index.html

www.ingramcontent.com/pod-product-compliance
Lightning Source LLC
Chambersburg PA
CBHW060210290526
45789CB00003B/1226